Nick meets the Man in the Wheelchair

Written by Rich E. Noll

Illustrated by Anne Harvey

Dedicated to Julia Noll

for helping me to experience my childhood again.

"Nicholas hold on to mommy's hand.
I don't want you to get lost."

The mall was busy on Saturday.
Nick and his mom joined the crowd.
They made their way past a shoe store
and then past a game store.

Nick stopped in front of the toy store's big display window. In the
window with its arms open wide, looking as though it was getting
ready to give someone a great big hug, was a red stuffed animal,
the same one he had asked his parents for over and over again.

Just then a man in a blue business suit exclaimed, "Whoa, watch it kid!" Nick's mom turned back towards the commotion.

Looking up, the man's face reminded Nick of the "big bad wolf"
in the story "Little Red Riding Hood."

"Nicholas!" his mom exclaimed.
Her cheeks flushed, attempting to
apologize as the man gathered himself, mumbling
under his breath. "Please be careful Nick,"
his mom said to him.

"Mommy, can we please go to the book store,"
he said pointing to the big letters that spelled BOOK STORE.

7

Nick entered the store with his mom in tow.
Rounding one of the bookshelves on his way to the
children's books, Nick froze in his tracks.

A man in a metallic blue wheelchair stared up
at the highest bookshelf. (One, two, three, four, five!)
Nick counted the shelves to himself as he watched intently.
Nick knew all sorts of people used wheelchairs.
His grandpa uses one. But this chair was VERY
different from the one his grandpa used.
First of all, it was much smaller and it was painted
a bright color, not the plain metal color he had
seen people use where his grandpa lives.
It also had rollerblade wheels in the front
instead of the large round gray tires
on grandpa's chair.

The man sensed his audience…

Nick's mom had finally caught up with him, walking into the situation. She understood why he had suddenly stopped. The two adults

smiled as a sign of acknowledgement. "Miss, would you mind reaching that book up there, the one with the blue cover?" he glanced back at Nick's mom briefly.

She smiled and stepped in front of him and
ran her hand down the row of books. "This one?" she asked.

"Yep, that's the one," the man replied.

"Thanks," he said again. Now he turned his attention to Nick.

"I bet you and I have the same problem.
We can't reach the tallest shelves."
The man paused and then spoke again,
"What's your name?"
Nick at first didn't realize that
the man in the wheelchair was
talking directly to him.

Once Nick realized the man was speaking to him,
he slipped behind his mom's legs. Nick's mom patted his head.
"Tell this nice man your name," she said to her son. "Nick!" he said
after a moment. "Mommy, why is the man in the wheelchair?"

Nick's mom blushed as she knelt down beside her son. "Well Nick, some people's legs are not strong enough to let them stand and walk so they need to use a wheelchair. Instead of using his legs, he uses his arms to get around."

"Your mom is right," the man interjected,
as he patted the wheels at his sides.
"These are my legs," he said. Nick spoke up again,
"Can you go really fast in that mister?"
The man smiled, "Pretty fast, but I have another
wheelchair that I use for racing and that one
can go as fast as some cars."

"Do you like sports cards?" the man asked.
Nick's eyes widened. He nodded excitedly. "Well,
can I give you my own card?" he spoke to Nick while
also glancing up to his mom for approval. She looked at
Nick with a smile, "That's nice of him, isn't it Nick."

Nick looked down at the card. He could not believe his eyes.
The man spoke up, "That's me downhill skiing
on what is called a 'Mono-ski.'"

Nick's mom and the man spent a few minutes talking
to each other while Nick continued to admire his new possession.

Nick's mom glanced down at her watch.
"Nick, we really should be going," she said to her son.
"Please say goodbye to…" she paused realizing she had not asked for his name nor had she shared her own.
"Sam," Nick spouted out glancing up to his mom showing her that his name was on the card.

"Well it was very nice to meet you, Nick," Sam said.

"You too, Sam," Nick replied.

As they walked through the mall, Nick turned to his mom and said,
"Mom, I'm going to show this to dad when he gets home tonight."
"That is a great idea honey," his mom said.

That night Nick waited by their big glass picture window watching for
his dad's car to come up the street. Soon a pair of car lights came down
the road, and Nick raced to the front door shouting, "Dad's home!"

Nick held the card tightly in his hand, watching for the door to open.
As the doorknob started to turn, Nick blurted out,
"Dad, dad look what I got!"

Nick's dad barely got
in the doorway as his
son started flapping the
card at him.

"Whoa, buddy," his dad
said kneeling down.
"Who is this?" he asked
looking up at his wife
who was in the kitchen making dinner.
She grinned looking at the scene of her husband and son.
"It's Sam," Nick responded, "Look what he can do."

Nick's dad looked at the card.

"That's pretty neat," Nick's dad said.

"He uses a wheelchair. Mom helped him get a book that was up on a really high shelf," Nick rattled off.

"Sounds like Nick learned a lot today," Nick's dad said to his wife. "It was pretty amazing to hear what Sam is able to do even when he is disabled. He is sure an inspiration. I'm really glad we met him today. He invited us to a basketball game that he will be playing in town," she said.

That night when Nick's mom went in to tuck
her son into bed she saw Sam's card carefully laid
out next to his bedside. She kissed her son on the
forehead and said, "Goodnight Nick. Sweet dreams."
She flipped off the light as she walked out of the room.

About the author:

Rich Noll lives in Rochester, Minnesota.
He is married to his wife Jill, and has a daughter
Julia to whom this book is dedicated. In his free time,
Rich enjoys fishing, doing crossword puzzles, word finds,
and reading. He initially wrote this story for a fiction class that
he was taking in college. It wasn't until after his first child
was born that he decided to finish the story.

About the illustrator:

Anne Harvey resides in Merriam, Kansas, with her husband and two kitties.
When not reading and illustrating, she teaches elementary school.

Made in the USA
Middletown, DE
27 May 2017